NORTH H
2

North Hampton, NH 03862
603-964-6326

OPOSSUM

Tom Jackson

Grolier
an imprint of

SCHOLASTIC

www.scholastic.com/librarypublishing

Published 2008 by Grolier
An imprint of Scholastic Library Publishing
Old Sherman Turnpike, Danbury,
Connecticut 06816

For The Brown Reference Group plc
Project Editor: Jolyon Goddard
Copy-editors: Tom Jackson, Cécile Landau
Picture Researcher: Clare Newman
Designers: Jeni Child, Lynne Ross,
       Sarah Williams
Managing Editor: Bridget Giles

Volume ISBN-13: 978-0-7172-6274-8
Volume ISBN-10: 0-7172-6274-X

**Library of Congress
Cataloging-in-Publication Data**

Nature's children. Set 3.
    p. cm.
    Includes bibliographical references and
index.
    ISBN 13: 978-0-7172-8082-7
    ISBN 10: 0-7172-8082-9
    1. Animals--Encyclopedias, Juvenile. 1.
    Grolier Educational (Firm)
    QL49.N384 2008
    590.3--dc22
                      2007031568

Printed and bound in China

PICTURE CREDITS

Front Cover: **Superstock**: Superstock Inc.

Back Cover: **NHPA**: Rod Planck;
Photolibrary.com: Alan and Sandy Carey,
Tom Lazar; **Shutterstock**: Alan Gleichman.

Alamy: E.R. Degginger 26–27, Don
Despain/www.rekindlephoto.com 13, Mark
Graf, 29; **Ardea**: D. Burgess 46; **Corbis**:
W. Perry Conway 41, Joe McDonald 17,
Lynda Richardson 34; **FLPA**: Jim
Brandenburg 30, S., D., and K. Maslowski 22,
45, Konrad Wothe/Minden Pictures 10, 33;
Nature PL: Lynn M. Stone 9; **NHPA**: John
Shaw 14; Photolibrary.com: Alan and Sandy
Carey 2–3, 37, Mark Hamblin 4, 21, Gordon
and Cathy Illg 42; **Still Pictures**:
BIOS/Thierry Montford 18, John Cancalosi
38, S. J. Krasemann 6, Tom Vezo 5.

Contents

FACT FILE: Opossum

Class	Mammals (Mammalia)
Order	Marsupials (Marsupiala)
Family	American marsupials (Didelphidae)
Genera	19 genera
Species	92 species, including the Virginia opossum (*Didelphis virginiana*)
World distribution	North America and South America; other marsupials live in Australia and New Guinea
Habitat	Forests, woodlands, fields, gardens, and parks; damp areas are preferred; some South American opossum live in streams
Distinctive physical characteristics	Long, thin tail and hairless, pink nose and ears; most female opossum have a pouch on their belly
Habits	Most are active at night; the Virginia opossum is a skilled climber and swimmer; sometimes play dead if captured by a predator
Diet	Small animals, including insects, and fruit

Introduction

Opossum are one of the most remarkable animals in North and South America. Many look similar to familiar animals, such as mice and raccoons. Like squirrels, opossum are expert tree climbers. They often hang upside down from tree branches. The opossum's closest relatives are kangaroos, koalas, and possum, which live thousands of miles away in Australia and New Guinea. Like their faraway relatives, female opossum raise their young in a **pouch** on their belly.

The Virginia opossum of North America is about the size of a cat.

A mother opossum
carries her young
around for the first
three to four months
of their life.

Hitching a Ride

Baby opossum travel in style. When they are very young, their mother carries them around in the cozy comfort of her pouch. When the young outgrow the pouch at about the age of six weeks, they ride on her back. Opossum mothers have large families. It can get crowded when all of the young cling to their mother's fur. She often curls her tail over her babies to keep them secure. The young opossum will soon be too large for her to carry. They will then have to take care of themselves.

White Animal

The word opossum comes from the Native American word *apasum*, meaning "white animal." This name refers to the most common opossum in North America: the Virginia opossum. This type, or **species**, of opossum lives mainly in the eastern United States. It is now, however, becoming more common all over the United States and also in southern Canada.

The Virginia opossum does not look anything like any other North American animal. It could almost be described as a white rat that is as big as a cat. Like a rat, the Virginia opossum has a long, pointed snout with a hairless pink tip. The long tail is also almost naked, like a rat's tail. However, an adult male opossum weighs 13 pounds (6 kg) and is between 24 and 32 inches (60–80 cm) long from nose to tail. Female Virginia opossum are slightly smaller.

The Virginia opossum is an adaptable animal. Its range has spread greatly in the past 100 years.

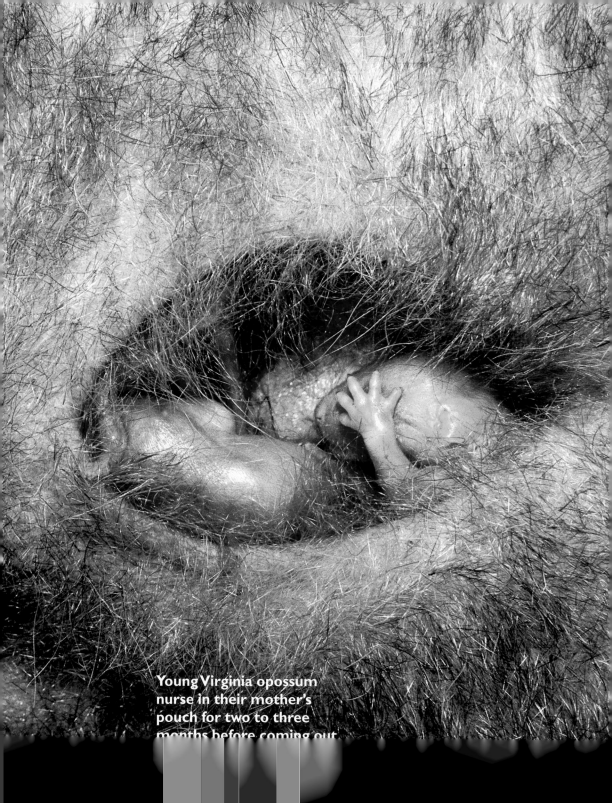

Young Virginia opossum nurse in their mother's pouch for two to three months before coming out.

Pouched Creatures

Opossum are **marsupials**. Most female marsupials have a pouch, or a fold of soft skin, on their belly. Their young are **nursed** and kept warm inside the pouch.

Marsupials are a very old group of **mammals** that appeared about 200 million years ago. At that time, giant dinosaurs ruled the world, but eventually they died out. Marsupials are still around, however. There are two groups of marsupials. The opossum are American marsupials. Most of them live in the forests of Central America and South America. The largest opossum is the Virginia opossum, which is the only one that lives north of Mexico.

Most of the world's marsupials live in Australia and New Guinea. Those include kangaroos, wombats, and koalas. Although America's opossum are sometimes called possum, they are not closely related to the possum of Australia.

At Home Anywhere

Many animal species are in danger of dying out. The animals are being forced to live in smaller and smaller areas. Eventually, there might be no room for them at all. It is the other way around for the Virginia opossum. This mammal is one of the few animals in the world that is actually becoming more common.

A hundred years ago, opossum lived in the swampy woodlands of the southeastern United States. Since then, they have gradually spread north. Today, opossum live as far north as New England, Minnesota, and across southeastern Canada. People have also introduced opossum to the West Coast. They now can be found from California up to British Columbia, Canada.

Opossum live on the edge of forests. They like to be close to streams or swamps. Opossum also happily make their home in towns or cities, usually in gardens and parks. They survive on waste food left in garbage.

A Virginia opossum
searches for food in
a backyard.

The Virginia opossum can see some colors but not as many as humans can.

Touchy Subject

Opossum are most active in the dark. Their sense of sight is not that good, so they rely on other senses to find out what is around them. Their naked ears can swivel to pick up faint sounds coming from different directions. The damp pink nose leads to an air chamber inside the long snout. The chamber is lined with millions of tiny detectors that can pick up thousands of different scents.

Opossum also rely on their sense of touch to find their way at night. They use their long tail to feel objects behind them. The tail is hairless to make it more sensitive. The snout is covered in many long whiskers. There are also whiskers on the forehead and cheeks. Whiskers act as feelers. They brush against branches and leaves as the opossum moves around. If the opossum can poke its head through a hole without it touching any of the whiskers, the animal knows that the hole is large enough to fit the rest of its body through.

On the Prowl

Opossum eat just about anything. That is why they are able to live in most areas. They have learned to knock over garbage cans to retrieve the leftovers inside. In the wild, opossum eat a lot of small animals. The opossum sniff them out in the dark, waddling along with their pink nose close to the ground. They prefer insects, such as crickets, beetles, and moths. However, opossum will also eat worms, snails, salamanders, frogs, and lizards. They catch many of these prey in trees. Up there, opossum also raid birds' nests to eat the eggs or chicks. Occasionally, Virginia opossum hunt larger animals, such as mice, moles, rabbits, and squirrels.

Rabbits are the largest animals that an opossum will kill and eat.

The gray four-eyed opossum from South America gets its name from the white patch above each eye.

Looking for Plants

The Virginia opossum has more teeth than any other marsupial. Its mouth contains 50 small teeth. All of them have sharp pointed tips. These teeth can crush up any type of food. As well as animal prey, opossum also sniff out fruit. They pick up berries that have fallen on the ground. If it cannot find enough food on the ground, an opossum will climb into a bush and feast on the fruit. In the southern United States, Virginia opossum are especially fond of persimmons and pokeberries.

Opossum find their food in a **home range**. Most home ranges are about 12 acres (5 ha). That's about the size of four soccer fields. In winter, when there is less food around, opossum wander over a much larger area to find enough to eat.

Furry Coat

An opossum's shaggy coat is made up of a mixture of white and black hairs. As well as being different colors, the hairs are also different lengths. The fur grows in two layers. Long white hairs stick out to give the opossum its spiky haircut. These are called **guard hairs**. They form a protective layer over the inner coat. That is made of shorter, curly hairs. This **underfur** forms a warm, woolly blanket around the body. The guard hairs help keep the underfur dry and clean. Many of the underfur hairs have black tips. When these mix with the white ones, they produce the opossum's silver-gray coat.

A Virginia opossum does not
have gray fur but a mixture of
white and black hairs.

An opossum's paws have sharp claws that help them grip when climbing.

Finger and Thumb

It may sound odd, but opossum have feet on their front legs and hands on the back legs! Just like human hands and feet, opossum's **paws** have five fingers and five toes. The toes point forward on the front paws, making them look like feet. One of the fingers on each rear paw sticks out to the side. That makes it look like a thumb, and so these hind paws work in the same way as a human's hands. The thumbs can move across the paw and be used to grip branches. That makes the opossum an excellent climber.

Twist in the Tail

The opossum has a "third hand" to keep it safe among the branches. The strong tail wraps around branches to hold on. Any hairs on the tail would make it slip, so the tail is bare. A tail that can grip and grasp objects is known as **prehensile** (PRE-HEN-SUL). The tail grips so well, that small Virginia opossum can even hang from their tail. They do that to reach fruits hanging from thin branches. Larger opossum are too heavy to hang upside down. If they try to hang by just the tail, they might get a nasty bump as they fall to the ground!

Plod Out of Sight

Opossum may be expert climbers, but they are not so good at moving along the ground. Four-legged mammals walk by moving two legs at a time. Most use the front leg from one side and the back leg from the opposite side. However, opossum move two legs on the same side. As a result they cannot walk very well. They just shuffle along.

The opossum's short legs stop it from walking and running very fast. The world record speed for a running opossum is just 8 miles (13 km) an hour. That is about as fast as a jogger.

Catching an opossum is not as easy as it may seem. Even though they are slow movers, the animal's short legs allow it to duck out of sight almost anywhere. It might nip under a bush or squeeze into a hollow log or burrow. It might even dash up a tree to get away.

The Virginia opossum is the only
North American mammal with a

Making the Bed

Opossum rest in an underground **den**. But they do not bother to dig a burrow of their own. Instead they take over one made by another animal, such as a groundhog or skunk. The opossum wait for the previous owner to move out before they move in. Opossum also set up home in hollow logs, or under a porch or barn.

An opossum likes to make its home very comfortable. It lines the den with grass and leaves to make it warm and dry. An opossum will change its bed often and must collect new bedding regularly. First, it arranges a bundle of bedding with its mouth. It then pushes that under the belly. The flexible tail then bends under the body to pick up the bundle. The opossum then waddles home. Soon it will have a clean bed to rest upon.

Opossum do not all live underground. Some make their homes in hollow logs.

An opossum sets off across the snow to look for food during a break in the wintery weather.

Frosty Reception

Most species of opossum live in warm regions of South America. Only the Virginia opossum in North America has to survive the snow and ice of the winter months.

The Virginia opossum has many of the same features as the other species of opossum. These features make it hard for the Virginia opossum to cope with cold weather. For example, their ears and tail get very cold without any hairs to keep them warm. The ears and tail might get frostbitten. If that happens, the tips of the ears or tail turn black and fall off!

When it is really cold, an opossum stays in its den for weeks at a time. It survives without eating by living off the fat stored inside its body. It stored this fat during the summer, when there was plenty of food available. A lot of the fat is stored in the thick base of the tail.

Fighting Back

Opossum have a lot of enemies. They are often under attack from owls, foxes, and bobcats. These **predators** hunt for opossum at night. That is the time when an opossum is most often out looking for food. The hunters attack without warning. Waddling opossum are not able to run away. What does an opossum do to defend itself?

A cornered opossum must rely on its best weapons: its teeth. It opens its mouth wide to show the 50 sharp points and hisses a warning to its attacker. An opossum is not a small animal, but looking even bigger will help scare off an enemy. It raises its spikes out of its shaggy coat and stands tall on its little legs. The tail points straight up to add as much height as possible. If this is not enough to save its life, the opossum has one more clever trick left.

An opossum's small but sharp teeth can give a nasty bite.

Opossum can play
dead for anywhere
from one minute
to several hours.

Playing Dead

Have you ever "played possum"? To do it you need to lie perfectly still as if you were dead. That is exactly what an opossum does if it is about to be snapped up by a bloodthirsty hunter. The opossum collapses to the ground and lies there with its eyes open and tongue hanging out. That is enough to fool predators, like cougars or lynx. Most of them prefer to eat freshly killed prey. The hunters will generally choose to leave dead bodies alone.

The predator prods the opossum to check if it is still alive. But the opossum can play dead very well. Its breathing slows down and its heart beats less often, so it can lie completely still.

Time to Mate

Opossum live alone. They will keep out of one another's way for most of the year. Adult opossum only spend time with each other during the **mating season**. The timing of the mating season depends on where the opossum live. The opossum living in the south **mate** the earliest. They start in January and continue until August. Opossum that live farther north will not start to mate until later. They might wait until late March in southern Canada. The northern opossum wait because they do not want their babies to be born when the weather is still harsh and food is difficult to find. Most female opossum will have one **litter** a year. However, in the south they might have time to raise two families each year, one in January and the other in July.

Young opossum play together, but adults stay out of one another's way until it is time to breed.

A baby opossum is about the size of a housefly when it is born—but it will grow quickly.

New Arrivals

Most baby mammals grow inside their mother and are reasonably well developed at birth. However, baby marsupials do not spend much time inside their mother. Most of the babies' development happens after they are born, outside the mother in her pouch. Opossum mothers are not pregnant for very long—just 13 days.

Before giving birth, a new mother prepares her den with fresh bedding. She then gives birth to up to 20 babies. That might sound very tiring, but opossum babies are tiny. They are just half an inch long (14 mm). All 20 babies could fit on a tablespoon.

The First Journey

Newborn opossum have bright red, hairless skin. Their eyes and ears are barely visible, and the back legs and tail are just stumps. The front legs have developed, though, and they are equipped with long claws.

The babies are far too small and helpless to live in the outside world. They must get to their mother's pouch quickly. The journey is only a few inches, but the babies must drag themselves through their mother's woolly fur to reach her pouch. The mother helps by licking a slippery path through the fur to the pouch. The babies then drag themselves across the mother's belly using their long front claws. Once they get into the pouch, the babies need to rest and grow. They will not come out again for three months.

An opossum mother is used as a climbing frame by her young.

By the time the baby opossum emerges from the pouch, it looks like a miniature version of adult opossum.

Inside the Pouch

The opossum's pouch is lined with fur to make it warm and dry. The female controls what goes in or out. She can open and close the pouch by relaxing and tightening a muscle. An opossum's pouch has 13 **nipples** inside. Twelve are arranged in a horseshoe-shape. The 13th is at the center. Often more than 13 babies make the journey into the pouch. They must race one another to find a nipple. Each baby puts a nipple in its mouth and does not let go again for 60 days. The unlucky babies that cannot find a free nipple will not survive.

Growing Up

As with all mammals, a baby opossum is fed on milk through a nipple. It is able to swallow milk and breathe at the same time—something that nonmarsupials cannot do.

The baby grows very quickly thanks to its constant supply of milk. The little pouch soon gets a bit crowded as the babies take up more and more space.

The first hairs grow after 14 days and soon the back legs and tail are growing well. The baby is still helpless until the age of about 55 days. That is when its eyes first open and it starts to look around the pouch. Soon it discovers there is more to the world than a furry sac filled with its brothers and sisters. It wants to go outside!

A young opossum is lighter
than an adult, so it can
climb on thinner branches.

The young opossum
has a lot to learn
about life outside
of the pouch.

Making an Exit

To leave the pouch, the curious opossum must let go of the nipple for the first time. It then clambers out to the outside world. The baby is still weak and can only manage a few shaky steps. It does not go far from the safety and comfort of the pouch. Instead, it takes a ride on its mother's back. It holds on to her fur with its long claws.

The babies must go back into the pouch often to nurse on milk. Soon their mother begins to teach them how to find and catch food. Her young watch from her back as she sniffs out food. When they are strong enough, the young opossum will try that out themselves.

Living Alone

An opossum mother will nurse her babies for about 100 days. By this time the young are too big to all fit into the pouch at the same time. Instead, the young just poke their heads in to find a nipple. The rest of their body pokes out of the pouch in a tangle of legs and tails.

Once a baby stops drinking its mother's milk, it is ready to leave home and find its own den. The young do not make a long journey. Most of them will set up home close to their mother. They will also be neighbors with their brothers and sisters for the rest of their life. However, once they have left home, they will not spend time with the other members of the family. From now on, they will avoid one another just as they would a stranger.

At the age of eight months, opossum are ready to mate for the first time and start a family of their own. Few opossum live for more than three years, but they can have dozens of offspring in that time.

Words to Know

Den   A type of animal home.

Guard hairs   Long, coarse hairs that make up the outer layer of an opossum's coat.

Home range   The area where an opossum finds its food.

Litter   Young animals born together.

Mammals   Animals that have hairs on their body and nurse their young with milk.

Marsupials   A group of mammals whose females carry the young in a pouch until they are fully grown.

Mate   To come together to produce young.

Mating season The time of year during which animals of the same kind come together to produce young.

Nipples	Part of a mother's body through which her babies drink her milk.
Nursed	Fed on milk from the mother's body.
Paws	The clawed feet of an animal.
Pouch	The fur-lined pocket on the female marsupial, where the babies live until they are fully developed.
Predators	Animals that hunt other animals for food.
Prehensile	When something can grasp or grip. The Virginia opossum's tail is prehensile.
Species	The scientific term for animals of the same type that can breed together.
Underfur	A thick layer of short hairs that covers the skin underneath an outer coat of guard hairs.

Find Out More

Books

Jacobs, L. *Opossum*. San Diego, California: Blackbirch Press, 2003.

Kalman, B. *What Is a Marsupial?* Science of Living Things. New York: Crabtree Publishing Company, 2000.

Web sites

Opossum

animals.nationalgeographic.com/animals/mammals/opossum.html

Information about opossum.

Virginia Opossum

www.enchantedlearning.com/subjects/mammals/marsupial/Vaopossumprintout.shtml

Facts about the Virginia opossum with a picture to print.

Index